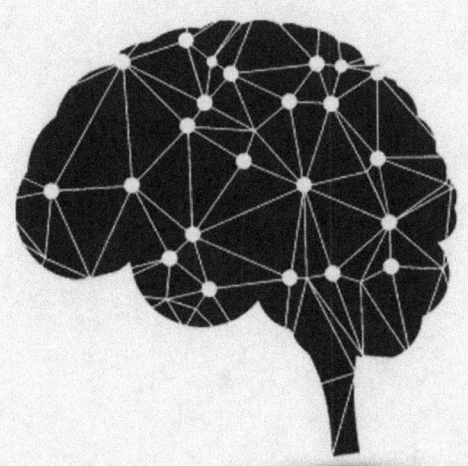

CREATIVITY COUNTS

IDEA-RICH CREATIVE
STRATEGIES

BOB 'IDEA MAN' HOOEY

AUTHOR, WHY DIDN'T I THINK OF THAT?

Dramatically improve your chances to succeed - revolutionize your performance and profitability!

Brainwaves, creative ideas, & notes...

Preface

Why is it some people seem to be more creative than others?

Why is it some companies seem to be leading on the creative edge?

For example:

Roy Speer and Lowell Paxson noticed people liked shopping and watching TV. The Home Shopping Network, a 24-hour shopping channel was launched.

Ole Evenrude got angry when the ice cream in his rowboat melted before he got to his island picnic spot – so he invented the first outboard motor.

Betty Nesmith noticed she made more mistakes with the newer electric typewriters in 1951. She invented a mixture of water-based paint and a colouring agent to help fix it. She sold her Liquid Paper Corporation to Gillette for $47.5 million in 1979.

Bob 'Idea Man' Hooey

Do you or your company have the creative spark to see and seize and idea when it pops up?

Can you harness the power of innovation to re-invent your future and build a more productive and profitable career or organization?

YES!

Then, read on my curious friend... "Curiousity is one of the foundations of creativity."

"Imagination is the beginning of creation. You imagine what you desire, you will what you imagine, and at last, you create what you will"
George Bernard Shaw

A word as we begin

I would like to begin by thanking you for allowing me to be a part of your career enhancement process. And, in allowing me to play the part of facilitator or creative '*nudge*' as you explore ways to tap into your creativity and apply some innovation in your day-to-day roles.

Exploring ways to increase your creativity and applied innovation is certainly worth your time. A worthy goal, and a challenging one, for sure. I am excited about exploring this idea with you.

Creative Partners' Andy Radka shared the results of a survey of 500 top American CEO's. They were asked what their organization needed to survive in the 21st Century? Their answer was, "***to practice creativity and innovation.***"

With our increasingly demanding environment, this would certainly make sense for business. How does it apply for crown or government agencies and non-profits? With increasing costs of living, other demands on the taxpayer and the government, it would make sense that finding ways of being more creative and using applied innovation would be of value.

Although that is not always easy to accomplish in the private or public sector.

Andy reported further on the survey "***only 6% of them believed they were tackling this effectively.***" Interesting gap isn't it? A challenge for us!

The important thing to focus your energies on, would be that **it is important and worth the effort to change the culture and introduce new innovative processes to your organization.** The other focus would be that **accessing creativity and using applied innovation is '*everyone's*' job.**

This is not just a role for a select few to investigate and report back to '*management*' for further study and eventual application. It is everyone's responsibility to remain open for ways to improve what they are doing in incremental steps as well as allowing their creativity to soar. It is when you capture ideas that you enhance your creativity. It is when you see those **Ideas At Work!** that you begin the process of innovation.

Note: You'll see a few of these Brain boosters throughout the book. Take a minute or two to warm up your brain and get your creative juices flowing. Write down your creative answers and come back to add to them.

Brain boosters: Give your mind a workout!

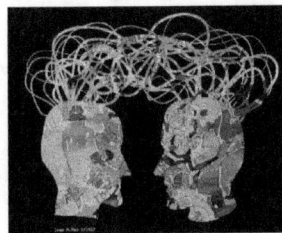

Spend 3 minutes looking around you and noticing everything you see that either has petroleum products in it or was made by use of petroleum products.

Computer technologists have just uncovered a new tool. It is called the "birdie." What does it do?

Assume you are blind. Close your eyes, reach into a drawer and pick up an object that you don't recognize. Describe it using your sound and touch senses.

Table of Contents

"Creativity is the quality that you bring to the activity that you are doing. It is an attitude, an inner approach – how you look at things . . . Whatsoever you do, if you do it joyfully, if you do it lovingly, if your act of doing is not purely economical, then it is creative." Osho

One percent better!

"Excellence results from doing 100 things 1 percent better, rather than one thing 100 percent better."
Author Unknown

One of the biggest obstacles to growth is the 'misguided' quest for the big idea, the big break, the big sale, or the big change. In reality, success, sales, and growth happen one step at a time, one improvement at a time, and often a simple, one percent-at-a-time.

Sure, there are many stories of major breakthroughs and advances; perhaps you've even experienced one or more yourself. However, when you look at what led up to them, you'll often see multiple efforts to improve, research, prepare, and experiment. This is often the case in my life and business as I work and prepare in advance of the successful completion or creative breakthrough.

It would be so easy if we could simply wait until the *big million-dollar idea* drops into our brains or laps and then simply reap the benefits. It would also be *unrealistic* to live that way. It would be like buying a lotto ticket as a means of paying your monthly bills. Top performers and leaders are never fully satisfied with where they or their teams are.

They have what many would call 'creative discontent' in that they can always see ways of tweaking or making it better. Many of the ones I meet or work with live this way.

Peters and Waterman (*In Search of Excellence*) wrote, *"The essence of excellence is the thousand concrete, minute-to-minute actions performed by everyone in an organization to keep a company on its course."*

Sam Walton of Wal-Mart fame was famous for looking at his competition with the eye of learning 'one thing' he could use to make what he and his team did a bit better. Sam Walton built a large, successful, multi-national company from a very little one by applying this concept of continuous improvement.

Jack Welsh made some amazing and profitable changes in GE by essentially doing the same thing.

What are your competitors doing better that you can apply?

Are there 10 to 15 areas where you can make changes that will give you a 1% improvement?

Write the ideas for improvement down and schedule specific time to make them happen.

One percent better can be your rallying call in the pursuit of excellence and success in your leadership, career, or company. Create and then change!

"Others have seen what is and asked why. I have seen what could be and asked why not."
Pablo Picasso

CREATIVITY

" Creativity has been built into everyone of us;
it's part of our design.

Each of us lives less of the life God intended
for us when we choose not to live out
the creative powers we possess."
Ted Engstrom

"Creativity is especially expressed in the ability to
make connections, to make associations, to turn
things around and express them in a new way."
Tim Hansen

"One of the major factors which differentiates creative
people from lesser creative people is that creative
people pay attention to their small ideas."
Roger von Oech

"We do not yet trust the unknown powers of thought."
Ralph Waldo Emerson

"Nothing is more dangerous than an idea,
when it's the only idea you have."
Linus Pauling

Creativity is a survival tool instilled at birth. However, it is a tool that needs to be 'enhanced,' 'honed,' and 'sharpened' as we move forward into life; more so as we enhance our career skills and roles as creative leaders, business owners, and top-level professionals. This little book gives you creative tools to do just that.

How to leverage *'Creativity Counts'*

'Creativity Counts' contains a range of tips, techniques, and ideas to help you improve the way you recruit, train, and lead your team for shared growth and long-term success. It evolved into its present form with the inclusion of stories, ideas, and first-hand experience based on copious conversations, notes, and observations of productive fellow leaders.

It has been updated (2023) with a focus to assist professionals and leaders to free up and better leverage their *creative* time to strategically invest in the lives and careers of those they lead. It is also designed as a timely guide for those who want to take personal leadership over their own lives and actions with a purpose of having their lives make a positive contribution.

This is not just a book for casual reading. It is a book to be 'chewed', to be dipped into, and leveraged as a resource or reference guide.

It is a **workbook** with homework; and, I hope, provocative questions that help you decide what you want to accomplish with your life, your business, your leadership, and your relationships. It is your resource, so mark it, highlight it, and make notes in the margins.

To get the best leverage from this idea-rich book, first visit the Table of Contents to identify which chapters and/or topics meet your most critical, time sensitive needs. Read them carefully and make sure you understand the guidelines and advice given. Some of the topics may not be of direct interest to you (now) depending on your needs. You may wish to read some of the other chapters so that you can understand the needs of other leaders or scenarios.

'Creativity Counts' does not contain ALL the answers. It is a collection of thoughts, notes, clippings, tips, techniques, lessons learned, and ideas shared primarily from one learner, one leader's viewpoint, mine.

It is simply intended as an aid to your reflection, learning, and inspiration – a resource that you can draw upon in preparation for your personal leadership endeavors. Its aim is to give you a creative resource that, when applied and practiced with real teams, will help you develop and build both your confidence and competence as a leader.

A more productive approach would be to take the tips and concepts presented here and blend them with your own leadership style, personality, and creativity. Keep in mind your own time constraints and 'comfort zone as a leader, business manager, or professional', to generate unique and personalized ideas on how you can create, give, and improve your interaction and action with your teams.

Creativity Counts is designed to offer you flexibility in how you leverage it for your personal and professional use.

You can sit down for an hour or two and read it **cover to cover**. This is a great way to start by getting a feel for what is included, especially for newer or emerging leaders who want to gain the full benefit from their investment.

 A word of advice: *'Creativity Counts'* is the result of over 29 plus years of personal study and first-hand experience in a variety of business leadership, coaching, and support roles for executive clients and their respective teams. It might seem overwhelming or confusing at first with the range of information included here.

Once you have done a quick read of the whole book, identify particular sections or tips that interest you and work on manageable chunks. You can select one chapter or section and work to incorporate the ideas you discover into your own leadership style and specific leadership role or personal situation.

You can look at the Table of Contents and jump straight to the tips or areas of study that particularly interest you.

We have attempted to incorporate something of benefit for everyone, regardless of your current level or skill in leadership. You might even find some contradictory advice in different parts of the book! This is because there is no single, universal 'right answer' – you must find what is a right fit for you, your objective, and your team's specific needs. What works for you is what is best. Choose it, try it, and adapt it as needed to serve you in your quest to be a more powerful and impactful leader and in taking control of how you allocate, invest, or leverage your time.

Brain Boosters: Give your mind a workout!

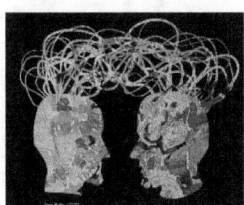 Research and common sense tells us that regular flexing of your creativity capacity will make it easier for you to be creative on demand. Have fun!

List as many antonyms (opposite meaning) for the word "narrow."

Close your eyes and write on a piece of paper. Write for a few minutes and try to do it without thinking. Then read or interpret what you have written.

While you are out on the streets today, notice how many people you see wearing hats. Count them.

Finish this sentence 20 times: People are most generous when _____.

Your 'Creative' Potential

"Ideas are the beginning point of all fortunes."
Napoleon Hill

In the short time we share here, I will attempt to kick-start your creativity and challenge your business *'mindsets'*, to help you look at what you do from a fresh perspective; to expose your senses to the opportunities which surround you. I've created this learning guide to give you some solid ideas to build on in pursuit of that creative quest.

To truly expand and **Unlock or Unleash Your 'Creative' Potential,** I'd suggest exploring a few ideas:

Learn to tap into your **Creative S.O.U.L.:** <u>S</u>eeker of wisdom; <u>O</u>penness to people and ideas; <u>U</u>nlimited energy; and a high <u>L</u>evel of risk and adventure.

Learn and apply the creative process to your situation:

Preparation;
incubation;
illumination;
and **implementation** on the creative thoughts.

Believe in your creative abilities. *Belief precedes creation!*

Don't be afraid to ask '*stupid*' questions. There aren't any!

Challenge your assumptions and existing mindsets.

Give your ideas breathing space to germinate and grow.

Read outside your normal zone to expand your mind. *(Try my books!* ☺ **www.SuccessPublications.ca***)*

Recruit a creative, collaborative circle of friends and fellow seekers.

Travel and be open to explore and expand by truly seeing new ideas.

Learn to explore the World Wide Web. Visit us at: **www.ideaman.net**

Make a conscientious effort to capture, record and save your ideas. See your **Ideas At Work** by using the four critical building blocks:

Planning;
Passion;
Persistence;
and of course; the **Patience** to see it through!

Remember to have fun! We learn best in times of enjoyment.

Use **"Thunder-thinking"** (brainstorming) to get thinking outside your box.

Create a special place that sparks and supports your creativity.

Share and expect synchronicity with the world.

Encourage idea volume generation with all your connections.

Just a few quick thoughts that might help you crank up the volume and burst your locked in *'business'* bubble, access your creativity and start applying innovation to your operations.

As Jacob Bronowski wrote, *"The world can only be grasped by action, not by contemplation... The hand is the cutting edge of the mind."*

Ideas in your mind need to be put into practice for the innovation to take root – **Ideas At Work!**

The Six Creative Indicators

Can you tell who is more likely to be a creative addition to your team? Can you separate the 'really' creative from the herd? Well according to research there are six basic indicators that might help in your quest to attract creative people for your team. People who rank high or exhibit more of these characteristics tend to be more creative.

Idea volume and fluency

This is an area where volume 'actually' counts. It may take 30 average ideas to yield one great one. Creative people tend to be better at generating ideas, even if most of them have little long term or applicable commercial value. Our minds are very much like a 'muscle' in that we tend to work better when we warm them up. They work better when they are exercised on a regular basis too. Our best ideas often come after we have worked through the more basic ones.

Slow to jump to conclusions or judge

You tend to get more high-quality ideas when judgment is withheld. This is the secret to effective brainstorming or 'Thunder-thinking'. Judging cuts off the creative flow of ideas. Judging tends to look for what doesn't fit or won't work verses exploring possibilities and potential. Creativity is willing to explore the options and potentials.

Imagination and flexibility

Creativity in its essence is based on flexible thinking. Creative people tend to exhibit almost a kid-like curiosity about life. Acting as if the world can be as you imagine enhances your creativity. *"The best way to predict the future is to create or invent it."*

Concentration and focus

Both of these traits are 'critical aspects' of creativity. Concentration is staying focused on a particular subject, even when you are tired, bored or frustrated. Creative behaviors are able to ignore or tune out distractions and outside stimuli while working to solve a problem or reach a goal.

Able to deal with ambiguity

Creativity is dealing with the vague and unformed to create the clear and concise. Creative people tend to be able to handle ambiguity where there is no clearly defined right or wrong. Creative people have a willingness to see all sides of a situation and to remain in questioning mode rather than rushing to find the answer. They keep going past the 'first' right answer to explore for the 'best' answer or innovative solution.

Able to handle disorder

Creative people tend to handle or even prefer disorder. Forget the stereotype of the absent-minded professor with stacks all around the office. This may be valid, but **disorder is not necessarily 'mess'**. Disorder refers to non-linear thinking, shaking up the normal order, status quo, or non-symmetrical design.

Keep these six indicators in mind when you are looking to recruit a member of your Mastermind Alliance, sales and marketing team, or support team. People do exhibit their creative traits if you are willing to look at and analyze their behaviour. Remember we can unleash our creativity, too.

I have sprinkled brain boosters and creative ideas for your fun throughout this book! Stop and play with them!

Ideas that are weird – perhaps?

Innovation and idea generation are, at the very basics, about being curious and courageous; curious about life, courageous about challenging the status quo, and then making changes to make it better.

This is where those who lead creatively excel. They are not afraid to go outside the confines of their narrow field and to borrow, beg, and sometimes 'steal' ideas from other fields and industries.

Great ideas are transferable! It is a good management practice to look at your 'norms' and ask yourself the 'contrarian' or flip side of the equation questions. This is where innovation and the real creative spark exist. That doesn't mean you always throw away what you are currently using. At times it is still very effective and may be the most productive use of your time, resources, and energy.

What if there is a better way, a more productive way, a more cost-effective way, and your competitor finds it first? Hmm?

The secret to thriving in our competitive, and by now everyone understands globally competitive market, is being constantly on the 'improve' and sometimes that means 'improve' to find the answers to the questions your existing and potential clients are asking. So keep questioning and keep on the quest to tap into your creative genius!

Brain boosters: (take a minute and let your brain play with one or two) Warming up your brain to engage your creative genius works!

Design the cover for a new book called, 'The best things in life are creative'!

Create 5 new brand names for a line of lady's watches. Men's watches.

What if birds barked and dogs chirped? What would that be like?

Change is a creative choice

In life, we have the opportunity to make changes. A death, a major illness, **or a major economic upheaval** can force us to take stock of our lives at that point and make some radical changes. In our changing economy, we find businesses, and government agencies being stretched and tested. Staffing has become more challenging, so has training and marketing. Customers are becoming more demanding and specific in what they want.

Change is pushed on us everywhere we turn. We can't avoid change, can we? That's what too many business owners think and miss their full potential.

Isn't it better to seize the opportunities to change and grow? Isn't it better to be someone who is open to learning, to stretch, and to push yourself past your comfort zone?

This change is a creative choice! Life is a series of changes and choices; why not control their direction and pace?

"Searching for the peak performer within yourself has one basic meaning -- You recognize yourself as a person who was born, not as a peak performer but as a learner. With the capacity to grow, change, and reach for the highest possibilities of human nature, you

regard yourself as a person in process. Not perfect, but a person who keeps asking: What more can I be? What else can I achieve that will benefit my organization and myself?" Charles Garfield

Ask yourself a few questions. Allow your honest reactions to reflect the changes in your attitudes, and actions that may need to be addressed to maximize your life and dealings in relation to your role at work.

What do I really want to have my life accomplish?

What is my biggest dream?

What would I like my team, company or organization to accomplish?

Where do I want my career to go?

What am I afraid of? What is stopping me? What keeps me up at night?

What do I need to change to make it work?

When do I need to change it?

When will I commit to start making these changes?

Will you have the courage to change? Will you commit to being your best, and to creatively build your organization to maximize its potential?

Remember the words of retailer J.C. Penney: *"No one need live a minute longer as he/she is, because the creator endowed us with the ability to change ourselves."*

Answering these questions will have given you a glimpse of what needs to be changed to make your dreams and goals a reality. The secret is in putting foundations under your dreams and actions under your goals.

The secret to **unlocking your 'creativity' potential** is in accessing your ability to embrace and utilize change for mutual benefit. **The choice is yours!**

"Great minds discuss ideas. Average minds discuss events. Small minds discuss people."
Henry Thomas Buckle

Creativity is 99% perspiration and 1% inspiration
Who said it was going to be easy?

Bryan Mattimore's excellent book on creativity, **"99% perspiration"** should be in your organization's library. It should be signed out and being *'worn out'* and re-read by your team.

Our ongoing success and survival in business is directly dependent on our creative ability to profitably solve the problems in our client's lives and operations. We use our *innovative solutions* to help make their lives and businesses better. Accessing or tapping into our creativity can be hard work unless you systemize your approach with great discipline.

We hear stories of the *'ah-ha'* **moments** in history, business, and science. These 'lightning bolt' occurrences nominally come about after many hours of research and applied study into a particular topic.

I know that is how it usually works in my writing and program creation activities. I research, read my brains out, and take copious notes before I start writing. They sometimes are *'mined'* from lessons drawn from past failures. Consider Thomas Edison and the 1000's of attempts to find a sustainable material for the filament for a light bulb.

Take the time to conduct systematic and well-rounded research, coupled with learning from your errors and mistakes. This will help fill your mind with the raw materials necessary for creative process development. This is, as you guessed, the *'perspiration'* part of the creative process and takes an investment on your part.

During the *'incubation'* period, let your subconscious mind chew on all this material and let it forge new connections with seemingly unrelated bits of information. Your subconscious will then send these vague feelings or intuitions to the surface or conscious mind.

The creative person has learned how to capture these thoughts, however vague, impractical, or wild, for later evaluation and analysis.

Be open and accessible to all ideas – regardless of size

I've seen many people fall to the trap of waiting for the *'big idea'* – a completely novel idea for a product, project, or service. They sit and wait for sudden inspiration or brilliant flashes of insight. Focusing on big ideas, we can easily become blinded from seeing smaller, otherwise *'good'* and *'valuable'* solutions.

Like the story I heard of an employee in the mailroom who noticed several packages being couriered to the same address. He checked into it, compiled them into one package with instructions on distribution at the receiving end. His 'small' change in process saved his company 1,000's of dollars each year.

While not as flashy or showy, these smaller insights and ideas often represent very workable and profitable options. Some can even lay the foundation for other great ideas.

Encourage your team to capture or share their ideas with you and investigate all the options contained. Consider that the original idea for the $1 billion dollar a year Levi Strauss Dockers line came from one of their employees in Argentina (who worked on the loading dock).

Time to sweat – perspiration activities

What can you do to fertilize your mind for enhanced brainstorming, or thunder thinking, as I like to call it? (Thunder thinking – when lightning strikes!) What kind of research or mental preparation or *'perspiration'* activities will help?

Suggestions that have successfully worked for me and other creative thinkers:

Visit authoritative web sites and learn to use search engines to conduct online research

Challenge your existing assumptions and mindsets. No sacred cows!

Remember to have fun! We learn best during times of enjoyment.

Use Google's news alert program to keep you informed on selected areas (other search engines and web-based programs will provide this type of material often daily.) I have several news topics on leadership, creativity and innovation and get emails with links to those stories daily.

Read books and magazine articles on the issue of topic you are studying or researching. A copy of my **'Why Didn't I THINK of That?'** might be a good addition to your library. **Visit: www.SuccessPublications.ca**

Map out the information you need, and potential sources where you might find it and ask open-ended questions to elicit the most usable and rich information.

Ask carefully crafted questions of experts in your study. They will often be able to kick start your creativity and give you a heads up that will advance your process to the next level.

Don't be afraid to ask seemingly stupid questions – there aren't any!

Learn to apply the **four-step creative process** to fully explore your ideas:

Preparation; incubation; illumination; and **implementation**.

Kraft Dinner – now you're cooking!

The story behind this decade-by-decade best-seller, as I learned it, happened following the war when Kraft Foods had pallets of their powered cheese packages (used by servicemen during the war) sitting 'unsold' in warehouses across the country. One east-coast manager was 'actually' selling out and headquarters sent someone to find out his secret.

As I heard the story, he creatively took the powered cheese packages, bundled each with a package of pasta and called it **Kraft Dinner**. Love the story and the creativity behind it. What do you have and what can you combine with it to make it more attractive or appetising to your clients?

The 21st Century version of the 3 R's

Most innovations are not *entirely* new creations; in fact, many represent new combinations or modifications of existing services, products, technologies, or materials.

I've been able to do this in some of my writing and programs in drawing from previously done programs or my writing in the creation of something more adapted or relevant to my audiences. In fact, this little book draws on some of my other works.

Secret hint: Don't re-invent the wheel each time but taking it a step up in the development of its use and scope.

Fortunately, word processing and computers, and visual outlining or diagramming programs make it easier to gather, analyze and manipulate information fragments into new combinations or versions.

This allows you to apply the 3 Rs in your creative process.

Research, retrieve and record information.

Review and revise the information you gather.

Recombine or re-use ideas – make new associations between the idea fragments of information you've gathered.

A few thoughts...

With the right kind of preparation, any one of your team members can experience an a-ha moment. It takes training, but it is not something only an Einstein would be able to do. Properly applied, **each member of your team can accomplish it!**

A few final tips to help facilitate this creative process:

Know where to look for information. Love learning – become a sponge for information on your topic or field of study.

Develop the skills in asking incisive, well thought-out, open-ended questions that draw out the information, the insights, and the wisdom of those you approach.

Experiment with mind mapping or other right brain stimulation tools to map out your assumptions, questions, insights, concerns, and needs for more information.

During the interim between your 'Thunder-thinking' or brainstorming sessions, **remain open for additional insights.** Be a sponge starting with your industry or profession and flowing outward into cross-functional disciplines, business, social or other areas. The insight you seek may not be found in the place you live or work, but it is out there.

Cultivate an 'insight-outlook'. Be open to considering information, insights, trends, and other data mined from multiple perspectives and personal experience. Work to identify and understand the inferences, underlying trends or connections they may contain and how they might pertain or impact what you are working on in your study.

"Around here, however, we don't look backwards for very long. We keep moving forward, opening up new doors and doing new things, because we're curious... and curiosity keeps leading us down new paths." Walt Disney Company

Ideas At Work! –
Priming the creativity pump

Ever notice how some people seem to be more creative, innovative, or just plain '*lucky*' at discovering solutions or having ideas strike, just when they need them? Ever wonder how they do it, or if they were born that way? Wish you could be more creative? You can! It is an acquired skill.

There is a secret, '*actually a process*', which will allow you to access your '*diminished*' creative spark and start a flow of good ideas from which the great, innovative, breakthrough ones might be found. To put it simply, you need to **prime the pump**, and be aware of what is happening.

I went camping one August. A lovely place in Northern Alberta nestled beside a clear, cool lake with lots of trees and natural surroundings. Very rustic, and just what I was looking for in my quest to take a mental break from two demanding projects I was working on then.

When I say rustic, I mean rustic; **no** showers, two quaint out-houses, and a fire pit where all that was provided. Water was available via a pump located by the lake that was connected to a well dug 100 plus feet into the ground. It took a lot of pumping, lots of noise, action and sweat until a noise was heard coming deep from the earth. Water would gush out. Once flowing, it was easy to maintain the flow while you filled your water container.

Our minds are like that, deeper than we would expect and often the best ideas are located way down in our subconscious, waiting to be pumped to the surface. **Using your mental muscles is like priming the pump** and that is what starts the ideas or water flowing.

Being curious about what is happening around you, reading outside your field, asking questions, *'mining'* or digging into ideas that interest you – all prime the pump and feed the reservoir from which the breakthrough, innovative ideas you seek come from.

Creativity seems easy, and it can be if you are systematic at working your brain. Feed your brain the ideas, the challenges, the opportunities, and lots of facts, background, and other information and see what bubbles to the surface.

But how do you apply this at work?

Take note of some of the other creative people who share in the global market. Perhaps they can teach you something that would be of benefit?

General Electric, under Jack Welsh, for example, was famous for *'borrowing'* ideas from other sources. They were openly researching ideas that could be transferred to their operations and looked at their suppliers, competitors, their various divisions, and other companies in the market for inspiration. If they saw something that was working, they asked, **"Would this work for us to make us more efficient or more competitive?"** If the answer was 'yes', they would apply it as quickly as it could be put into action.

According to their own history they learned (from their own departments) about productivity from Lighting; quick response asset management from Appliances; effectiveness from GE Capital; bullet train cost reduction techniques from Aircraft engines; global accounting management from accounting.

Wal-Mart taught them direct customer feedback – quick market intelligence. They learned new product introduction from Toshiba, Chrysler, HP, Toyota, and Yokagaw. Ford and Xerox shared insight on launching quality initiatives.

What have you learned from your competitors, suppliers or even your own personnel lately?

Wal-Mart's success is not product specific. Sam Walton looked to others for ideas and was able to apply innovation in his various processes for doing business. Sam applied innovation in supplier relationships, distribution, location, and pricing. This allowed him to maintain a competitive advantage in supplying his customers with what they wanted, at a price they could afford.

General Motors was the first automobile manufacturer to introduce color to the product mix, which has had some long-lasting benefit for that industry and for us as consumers.

But did you know GE also invented consumer credit, which allowed people who'd never owned a car to be able to purchase one over time. (*Gee, only 133 more payments and it's mine.* ☺)

3M, famous for inventing the post it notes (and their champion had to fight to get them introduced as there was no demand at the time, or so the 'experts' said); has a 30/4 rule in place to encourage its employees to explore new ideas and processes.

Simply said, 30% of their sales need to come from products that are less than 4 years old. Keeps them fresh and keeps them priming the creativity pumps.

George **Westinghouse** ran into 'conventional wisdom when he suggested to a few railroad executives that a train could be stopped by using wind. His imagination was unstoppable. Westinghouse Air Brakes soon became conventional equipment on North American trains, and trucks too.

George de Mestral noticed the burrs he was brushing out of his wool pants and his dog's coat. He became curious about the tenacity of the burrs. A little observation under a microscope revealed hundreds of tiny hooks snagged in mats of wool and fur. Years later, he made a connection, and the invention of **Velcro ™ fasteners** was born.

Einstein would have been proud. Albert Einstein on creativity, said, *"To raise new questions, new possibilities, to regard old problems from a new angle, requires creative imagination."*

Three challenges emerge to priming your creativity pump:

Think things out fresh…be unconventional

Destroy the old, and then create new, where needed.

Tap your imagination. Consider new ideas, ask new questions, and raise new possibilities.

(the rest of the story) Ole Evinrude was in love and engaged to be married. One summer he rowed his fiancée, Bess across the lake to a little island for a romantic afternoon picnic. They had forgotten the dessert. Ole rowed back and returned with the dessert. About midpoint, tired, beat, and sweating under the sun and humidity, he stopped to catch his breath. Although the ice cream was melting, his creative processes were engaged. He said, **'There must be an easier way to do this?"**

This prompted the invention of the first portable outboard motor in 1906, with a commercially successful version in 1909. Ole got his patent in 1910 and went on to dominate the market for decades.

Creativity can strike when you least expect it. Keep priming the creativity pump and keep your eyes open. You might just surprise yourself and be revealed as a creative thinker!

"If I were not a physicist, I would probably be a musician. I often think in music. I live my daydreams in music. I see my life in terms of music." Albert Einstein

Business observations on applied creativity

When teaching this program in person I often pull examples from business to illustrate creative techniques. Many of these you know, but they still ring true.

For example, **Barbie** is a creative example of a product with a built-in add-on or up-sell capacity. She comes with one outfit, and you are encouraged to buy more and to accessorize her life. You can even buy her friends too. Interesting!

Dominos built a profitable slice of the pizza business by simply promising to get it there hot and ready to eat. This differentiated them from those cold and greasy competitors. What can you do to differentiate yourself from your competition? What can you create as your unique selling proposition?

Telus, AT&T, and the satellite or cable outlets taught how to take a basic service and bundle items clients want for a higher rate. What can you bundle?

Starbucks took an espresso machine previously seen in Italian and European coffee shops and built and empire around the world selling their 'experience'.

Canadian trapper, **Charles Birdseye** observed that the fish he caught during the winter froze quickly. When he cooked them, they still tasted fresh. This observant concept was the start of the frozen food industry.

Food for thought...
Feeding your Creative Process

Here are a few tips to help you feed your mind and fuel the creative process in your day-to-day role on the job. Use these as warm ups, or tune-ups to keep your mind fresh and alive.

Warm up your creativity - take two unrelated objects; Imagine comparisons or connections between them. For example, a diamond and an elephant. Both have different facets and come from Africa.

Practice mental pinball - Take one word or thought; See if you can freely associate 10 - 20 items or thoughts.

Look at other areas, worlds or industries to spark the solution you need - eg frequent flyer miles and coffee cards.

Creative environment – for example: casual clothes, warm room, soft couch, fireplace, soft music, walking outdoors on a lovely day, or working in a dimly lit room.

What would a famous person do? The Pope, Jay Leno, JFK, Mother Theresa, or... *(pick someone you admire for their creative abilities)*

Think 'POSITIVE' – ie, let's look at the *'workable'* parts.

Go for quantity if you want quality. Ideas beget more ideas! Pick the best ones from the bunch and save the remainder for another look.

Play to keep your creativity alive *(remember your child)*, explore and have fun with the challenge.

Solutions come when you least expect them - **relax!**

Team works - apply the power of collective thinking! Create a Success team or un-official team of advisors!

Information, time and the ability to solve problems creatively are the most valued currencies in business.

Learn to use technology, attend a seminar, listen to a tape, read a book, buy some re-active thinking software.

Being *'wrong'* is part of the creative process. To reach success - increase your failure rate: but don't fail to learn the lesson from the lesson!

Get past the fear of looking stupid.

Believe in 'YOU' as a creative source. Belief proceeds creation!

Don't let the negativity get to you.

Tackle your fears to unleash your creativity.

Just a few thoughts to feed your creativity muscles.

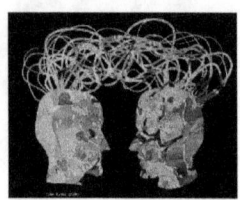

Mental exercise is a daily regimen and is just as important to your life as regular exercise and a healthy diet. You need to feed and exercise your mind if you want to be creative and discover the innovative solutions to your customer's needs.

These tips will give your mind what it needs to get into shape and keep into shape for creative application on the job and in your life in general.

"Think left and think right and think low and think high. Oh, the thinks you can think up if only you try." Dr. Seuss

Growing to the next level
(using innovation)

Is your organization stagnating? Are you finding it a challenge just to keep up with the regular demands made on your team? How do you keep growing?

Growing your people will result in growing your organization. Now there is a novel approach to success in business or any operation.☺ Making innovation an integral embedded process may just be the answer. After all, you have a process for almost everything else, don't you? **Prepare Yourself to WIN!** by investing your time and resources in equipping your team to creatively grow and succeed.

I came across a book by **Robert B. Tucker** a while back that shed some additional light and offers us some solid advice on how to do this.

In *'Driving growth through innovation,'* Robert outlines a synthesis of options based on what leading companies like Proctor & Gamble, Colgate-Palmolive, EDS, Royal Dutch/Shell and Citigroup are doing to encourage growth and earning rates thru applied innovation. In his book he describes how they have been able to bring new ideas to life for "greater speed, payback and more consistent momentum."

What sets these corporate role models apart is their ability to include everyone throughout the organization in the innovation process. They can uncover *unmet* client needs or desires, create and produce prototype ideas in a short time frame, and assess feasibility quickly.

Organic or inward growth will become more critical in the years to come. It will come from applied innovation, not cost cutting bottom line-oriented activities. These are always important, but they don't drive top line growth or sustain profitability. They will be counter productive, if not handled correctly.

Investing in innovation and teaching everyone on your team these principles of applied innovation, as shared by Robert B. Tucker, will bring you the desired ROI you seek, and perhaps the '*real*' top-line growth as well. *I include a few of his ideas along with my own thoughts.*

Tucker's Principles of Applied Innovation (and my insights)

Approach innovation as a discipline. Teach your team to think '***through***' their ideas and how to understand which ones are in alignment with your organization's visions, goals, mission statements or principles. Remember, you get better at something with practice, so encouragement works, even if the initial ideas need work. Show your team how to champion and sell their ideas, and where they can go (*hopefully to you*) for coaching and encouragement, and how to build creative coalitions of support.

Approach innovation comprehensively. If you want innovation to become an ingrained mindset in your organization, don't let it be confined to one department or an *'elite'* group of high performers. Work with your HR department to ensure that innovation performance is a part of every job description, and every manager or supervisor's evaluation.

Hire for this skill - beef up your innovation muscles and bench strength.

Promote from this perspective to send a consistent and positive message. Innovation must encompass new product development, services, training and development, processes, customer service, strategies, finance and business models, markets and distribution channels.

Innovation must incorporate a systematic, organized, and continued search for new opportunities and vistas to explore.

Promote a deeper understanding of social, demographic, and technological changes in your search for the possibilities in your future.

Why not challenge your team to become *'trend spotters'* who search for disruptive technologies, new innovations and inventions, and perhaps even wacky ideas that might contain the seeds of innovation you need? Mining the future from the minds of today!

Everyone in the organization must be involved in innovation. Ensure your team builds an *'idea management'* system to capture ideas from the rank and file, not just your management personnel.

Good innovative ideas often come from the fringe of your team, the ones you normally wouldn't ask, who see areas of improvement or new services but are too shy to share. Make it a point to draw out their input, insight and experience. They may have encountered something with a client that could provide the genesis of a new line or profitable service addition. *(My 'idea catchers' might be a start in this direction.)*

Innovation must be customer centered to be profitable. You can't always depend on the insights provided from your clients. Sometimes they don't know or recognize what they need or want until you show it to them. **A focus of innovation** to make their lives better, in service, in selection, in making it easier for them to do business with you, in how you handle their concerns, problems, and complaints will do wonders.

Creating value for the client is the only sure route to continued success. Client focused innovation is more profitable as it deals with the 'top-line' of your business. Innovation to shore up your bottom line also enables you to grow and put those '*liberated*' resources into growth, promotion and performance enhancement.

We cover more on that in '*Make ME Feel Special! Idea-rich customer service strategies*' available from **www.SuccessPublications.ca**

Listen to your clients, you might learn something that could provide a new or unconventional way of doing business and continuing to earn theirs. Use client feedback, focus groups and on-line forums to provide a venue for sharing of ideas, concerns, and feedback on performance issues.

Taking time to understand these principles of applied innovation will help your team develop a strategy for innovation to guide your organization thru good and bad times. A strategy that will help in surviving normal and eventual leadership changes.

Brain Boosters: Give your mind a workout!

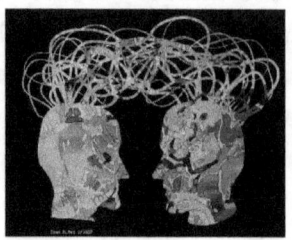

You are a band that plays New Age music.

What is your name and logo? Take a moment and draw a rough sketch of it.

Write five unusual Chinese fortune cookies.

A man runs into McDonald's and buys 40 of the newest toys that McDonald's is promoting. The man has no children, and it is in the middle of a workday. Why is he doing this?

"Creativity is allowing yourself to make mistakes. Art is knowing which ones to keep." Scott Adams

Innovate or evaporate –
The time to act is NOW!

When would be the best time to start some serious work on innovation in your organization? Now! Is the short answer.

The gap between imagination and achievement or actualization has never been shorter. Beginning '*somewhere*' is always preferable to waiting while your team weighs the options and while the organization goes bust or gets left in the dust by those competitors who are being innovative and creative in this volatile market.

Author of **"Leading the Revolution"** Gary Hamel advocates that '*radical innovation is the competitive advantage of the new millennium.*" With the aftermath of the past 18 – 24 months since 911, the Enron fallout, and a more recent general shake up in our economy a wake-up call is in order.

But that can be a challenge to productive change with some organizations mental constraints and stuck in the mud mindsets. J.K. Galbraith, noted economist once shared, "*Faced with the choice of changing one's mind and proving there is no need to – almost everyone gets busy on the proof.*" Everyone needs to be involved. Partial commitment to innovation is commitment to failure.

There needs to be a willingness to listen to, and act on, the change plan that comes from this innovation process.

Creative Partners' Andy Radka shares the results of a survey of 500 top American CEO's. They were asked what their organization needed to survive in the 21st Century? Their top answer was *'to practice creativity and innovation."*

However, **'only 6% of them believed they were tackling this effectively."** Quite a gap between needs and application. Obviously blending in a spirit of innovation takes time vs a quick fix or special seminar.

If innovation and creativity are so important, even critical in business survival, why the gap in application and implementation? While each organization is distinct and different, there needs to be a more holistic, integrated approach to innovation and creativity as a culture. We need to get 'buy in' on all levels. Further we need to consider some important points to increase the possibility of idea generation, which in turn drives innovation and creativity in an organization.

What can you do to facilitate this process? Here are some areas of concern in building a foundation for success under this creative and innovative initiative:

Innovation strategy: Innovation needs to be an *'integral part'* of all strategies and policies in your organization, not just *'tacked'* on as a quick fix up. It needs to permeate every department, every section. Every employee must make it a focus in part as they do their respective roles. For example, how much time is spent in the boardroom discussing ongoing innovation strategy? This is where the *'rubber hits the road'* and your employees see just how much you are committed to this path of action.

Support from top management: In too many organizations ideas and innovation steps are already at risk at their inception. Poor leadership can look the other way or take the courageous step and stretch out a helping hand to buoy them until they can be worked out and tried in the real world. Ask yourself, "Do my managers see themselves as leaders whose role is to *'clear the way' for creativity'* or are they simply status quo oriented?" Your employees and colleagues are watching for your leadership in this arena. What will they see?

Collective mindsets: Whether we acknowledge it or not, we each have mindsets comprised of beliefs, attitudes, and values that drive or motivate our behaviour. These collective mindsets (*e.g. 'can't teach old dogs new tricks' or 'my people aren't creative')* often form barriers to the creative process. They need to be unlocked and unblocked.

Business guru Peter Drucker once said, *"defending yesterday – i.e., not innovating – is far riskier than making tomorrow."* Make sure your organizational mindset is not creating an *'immune system'* or anti-virus system that automatically rejects or attacks new ideas, processes or challenges to the status quo business model. This can be your largest obstacle in embedding creative approaches and applied innovation within your organization.

Employees get needed tools and training: Are your staff given the tools and the on-going training they need to support a creative climate and innovation?

People and training are crucial to your success, and the training needs to be ongoing and reinforced. Creativity will not magically flourish with the advent of a few courses or the provision of a few creative tools to a few people. Everyone needs to be trained and supported in his or her evolution of understanding and applied learning.

Knowledge management tools: Does your organization have an intranet that capitalizes on the stride's information technology has brought to the battle for business survival? **IT often acts as an enabler,** which allows us to break the traditional barriers of function, geography and even hierarchy.

This allows for internet-based sparking of ideas and a chance to engage and bring 'all' the minds or your various teams into the game. This is how you win! (*For example, this year the Titleist people used 5 of my articles on a new intranet site being set up for their sales staff.*)

What gets measured gets done – metrics for innovation: Creativity and innovation can be measured and if so, are done on a more consistent basis. Creativity, when rewarded, is even more! Intellectual assets can impact heavily on your market value. Consider the differential and costs between hardware and software values.

Creation of an idea pipeline: Is there an effective innovation process, pipeline, or some form of tracking system for converting ideas into innovative services or new products? Is everyone on your team committed to feeding this process or pipeline? Only systematic processes, which incorporate a blend of logical and lateral, thinking tools can bring creativity and innovation. What are you doing to ensure you prime the pump and keep this pipeline full and flowing?

Supplier and customer mindsets: Organizations create a demand for innovative suppliers to be able to serve their clients who are demanding innovative products and services. Ask yourself, 'are your current (and potential) clients able to support a dialogue about inventing your shared future?

How about your suppliers and allied professionals? They may not even recognize the future until they see it or are made aware of its possibilities. That in part, is your job in the connection and education process of business.

Just a few thoughts to consider as you follow your quest to increased creativity and applied innovation in your organization.

The time to act is now! **Innovate or evaporate in the dust of those competitors who saw the need, made the investment, and took the lead.** It's your choice!

"Innovation is not a private act – it is seldom the product of a single individual's intellectual brilliance. Innovation is a product of the connections between individuals and their ideas... it is the constant interplay of ideas, perspectives, experiences, and values that spawn's innovation."
Gary Hamel

From 'KAI-ZEN' to 'I CAN!'
Improvement = Consistent commitment to good change

Kai = *change* Zen = *good*
Used together = *improvement*

Kai-zen came to North America in the mid 1980's, after becoming an integral part of the Japanese management theory. Western management consultants used it to embrace a wide range of management practices, which were regarded as primarily Japanese.

These practices were thought to be the secrets of the strength of Japanese companies in the areas of continual improvement rather than innovation. According to this theory, the strength of Japanese organizations lay in their **attention to '*process*'** rather than results. They also concentrated the team efforts to continually improve imperfections at each stage of the process. According to them, over the long term, the result was more reliable, of better quality, more advanced, and attractive to clients and less expensive than Western Management practices.

Its '*roots*' however are from an American influence following the 2nd world war. General Douglas MacArthur approached several leading US experts to visit Japan to advise them on how to proceed on rebuilding their country and their economy.

One such expert was **Dr. Edwards Deming.** He initially came over to conduct a census, but noticed the newly emerging industries were having difficulty. He had been involved in reducing waste in US War manufacturing and drew on that experience to offer his advice.

By the 1950's, he was a regular visitor, offering advice to Japanese manufactures that were having challenges in terms of raw materials, components, and investment; in addition, suffering from low morale in the nation and workforce. By the 1970's, many of Japan's leading organizations had embraced Dr. Deming's key points for management. Most are as valid today as they were a half-century ago.

Here are some I felt relate to the concept called Kai-zen.

An improved philosophy to effectively deal with change and client needs.

Constant pursuit of purpose required for improvement of products and services.

Improving every process for planning, production, and service.

Instituting or embedding on going, on the job training for all staff using a variety of methods and ideas.

Instituting and supporting leadership that is aimed and focused on helping people do a better job. *(Isn't that the true purpose of 21st Century leadership and management?)*

Breaking down the barriers and boundaries that exist within departments and people. *(GE's CEO, Jack Welsh took this one on personally in his style of management.)*

Encouraging education for the self-improvement of every member of the organization.

Top management is committed to improve *'all'* these points, specifically quality and leadership.

Adapting the Kai-zen attitude to our western way of doing business requires **a major change in corporate culture** – creating a corporate culture that:

Admits openly and honestly there are problems and challenges.

Encourages a positive, collaborative, consultative attitude to solving or overcoming problems or challenges.

Actively *'devolves'* responsibility to the most appropriate or effective level. The person who is in the best position to deal with the challenge or problem needs to have the tools and the authority to do so.

Promotes continuous skills-based training and development of attitudes.

Traditionally, the Japanese approach has embedded Kaizen in its hierarchical structural, although it gives substantially more responsibilities within certain fixed boundaries.

The **key features** of this management approach and focus are:

Attention to process, rather than results: Analyze every part of the process down to the smallest detail, with a view to improving them. Looks at how employee's actions, equipment and materials can be improved.

Cross-functional management: Management team has an expanded focus on helping improve the process and the skills of the people outside the typical western turf wars.

Use of **quality circles:** and other tools to support their commitment to continuous improvement.

A range of tools have been developed, along the KAI-ZEN line, to assist companies to make **tangible improvements**:

Quality Control Circles: groups of people whose primary focus and purpose is to continually improve quality.

Process-oriented management: more attention focused on the 'how' *(the process)* rather than the 'what' *(the task).*

Visible management: top executives are being seen, *'walking the job'* (management by walking around) and being available to *'see'* and consult on each stage of the process.

Cross-functional management: working across functional divides and typical barriers or boundaries, to provide more unity, sense of team, and a wider vision that engages and involves everyone.

Just-in-time management: control of stock, and other materials and components to avoid unnecessary expenditures.

PDCA: a process of **P**lan, **D**o, **C**heck, **A**ct to assist in solving problems or challenges.

Statistical process control: enable each machine operator or member of a team to control and measure quality at each stage of the process.

In the Japanese approach to Kai-zen, all of these tools are used in a holistic manner. **Contrast this to the current western approach**: where some of these tools are individually introduced as the *'answer'* to every problem or challenge, without consideration of the context within which they were designed to work effectively.

Some **perceived benefits** of this Kai-zen type of approach:

Can lead to a reduction of waste

Can increase productivity

Relatively easy to introduce – requires no major capital investment

Can lower the break even point
Enables organizations to react quickly to market changes

Appropriate for fast and slow economies as well as growing or mature markets

Some **challenges of introducing Kai-zen** into the western management mind-set are:

Can be difficult to achieve Kai-zen in practice, as it requires a complete or major change in attitude and culture. It needs the energy and commitment of all employees. It also requires a substantive investment of time.

Can be difficult to maintain enthusiasm for several reasons: some see Kai-zen as a threat to their jobs; poor ideas tend to be put forward along with good ideas, which can at times be de-motivating; by implication, there is never a complete satisfaction.

Continuous improvement is not sufficient or a stand-alone approach in itself. Major innovation is still needed. There is a danger on becoming *'evolutionary'* in focus to the exclusion of being *'revolutionary'* or innovation sensitive.

In this turbulent, global economy, organizations need to look seriously at any and all methods, tools, techniques and training processes that might help in this quest for growth. Kai-zen's step-by-step approach is in direct contrast to the great leaps forward many organizations experience via the innovation avenue.

It is almost as though we need to develop a *'bi-focal'* approach and viewpoint, which is one that encompasses steady, continuous improvement of current processes, products and services. At the same time looking for and encouraging creativity and innovation in moving the organization to the next level. *(I do this in the development of my programs and publications.)*

Kai-zen should free senior managers to think about the long-term future of the organization, look for new opportunities, and move to a concentration on *'strategic'* issues. Kai-zen can support improvement of *'existing'* activities; but it will not provide the impetus for the innovation process, which often provides our great leaps forward.

A **balanced approach** is called for here.

It is the role of *'strategic'* leadership to take responsibility for the implementation of an effective corporate mission *(purpose or soul)*, reward, and the organizational structure.

It is the responsibility of *'tactical and strategic'* managers to model and practice sound leadership, promote good teamwork, and to work to ensure everyone understands their roles and the process itself.

It is the responsibility of *'everyone'* in the organization *(from front-line to senior management)*, to measure themselves and their teams, to identify in quantifiable, measurable terms, areas for improvement, to generate ideas to change practice and procedures. Then to continue measurement to ensure this improvement has been achieved, recorded, and celebrated. *(Don't forget to celebrate the win!)*

Each time it is measured, it can be analyzed, and a new standard achieved or set and measured. This becomes the **cycle of continual improvement**.

Here is a typical or **suggested cycle or process**:

Generate ideas,

evaluate ideas,

decide on action,

plan implementation,

design measurement system,

take action,

set new standard,

measure, analyze,

define problem/desired state,

identify areas for improvement,

generate ideas… and continue cycle.

Everyone on your team needs to be '*totally*' committed to this cycle of continuous improvement. Each team member must be given the knowledge, skills, and tools to be able to participate fully and enthusiastically. To participate, not only within their own respective teams; but also, across the organization as a whole, as a part of a cross-functional team.

For this to become a reality, work must be done to reinforce or build the confidence within your staff to take on greater responsibility, or to make decisions for themselves. This is crucial to its success. In addition to specific skills training and use of tools and knowledge, it is important for us to work on the '***climate for change,*** to ensure it is embedded in our corporate culture.

The core values within a Kai-zen based approach to which each of us can aspire are:

Trust and respect for every member of the team across the organization, not just his or her own team. *(Not just their department, their own specialization, expertise, or level.)*

Everyone on a team should be able to **openly admit any mistakes** or failings they've made or exist in their role, and work on doing a better job the next time.

Responsibility is an individual commitment. **Progress is impossible without the ability to admit, learn from and move forward from mistakes.**

Many years ago, I listened to *'A Power Talk'* CD from Anthony Robbins, in which he shared his concept of Kai-zen for use in our day-to-day lives and roles as leaders. He was quite passionate about his commitment to this concept *(ok – when is he not passionate?)*, and for its implementation in our daily lives. He advocated a commitment to constant and never-ending improvement

I'd like to take a *'robins-esque'* approach, and challenge each of you to take a moment to digest what we've discussed about this transplanted US – filtered through Japan approach to management, as a part of your personal leadership role.

If you and your team are going to move successfully to the next level of growth, each of you will need to get a firm foundation and focus on the process of Kai-zen style continual improvement.

This is in addition to your personal leadership in applied innovation or **Ideas At Work**! - as they apply to your changing roles, direction, and the teams you seek to lead.

My challenge is for you: Develop an **'I CAN!' approach and attitude to your leadership,** and to equipping and inspiring those you would seek to lead. *'Improvement is continual and never ending,' and it starts with me!* Gee, that sounds like something I've heard, *"To the leading-edge leader, to the successful entrepreneur -- school is never out, and the education never ends."*

Enjoy the journey! After all, in the **'Kai-zen' or 'I CAN!' world**, the journey is the goal and provides the sense of achievement and satisfaction.

"Creativity is just connecting things. When you ask creative people how they did something, they feel a little guilty because they didn't really do it, they just saw something. It seemed obvious to them after a while." Steve Jobs

Picture this… the art of seeing photographically

While I was taking my architectural training in the 1970's I pursued the use of a camera to cover some of my education expenses. In addition to being the photo director for the college I took assignments for weddings, special functions, meetings, and other gatherings where *'capturing the moment'* was desired and valued by my clients.

I've been able to *'develop'* some of those skills as a photographer with my role as an **'idea man'** or creative catalyst for my clients and audiences. These skills have helped me to *'see'* with increased clarity in some of the other areas of my life, my business, and my interaction with those I serve. There are some interesting parallels between the skill of looking creatively thru the lens of a camera and the art or skill of creative problem solving or strategic planning.

Photographic creative elements. I suggest there are a number of creative elements that contribute to good photography, and they serve as metaphors for the world of creativity and innovation. Lens selection is just one of them.

Most 35mm camera bodies, including the newer digital ones, have interchangeable lenses, which allow us **to 'frame' our subject in a variety of interesting and creative ways:**

Normal focal length lens *(comes with the camera as a standard)* allows you to shoot pictures from a perspective very similar to what you see with your naked eye.

Telephoto lenses *(come in various combinations)* allow you to bring in distant objects by appearing to make them closer. They tend to focus in on one part of the scene and provide a decreased field of view than the normal lens.

Wide-angle lenses take in more of the scene that a normal lens. They tend to emphasize the distances between objects and sometimes distort a bit on the edges.

Panoramic lenses take in a full spectrum shot giving you the 'big picture' view. They tend to take more time, are more susceptible to movement distortion and use more film.

Lighting selection *(natural, augmented)*, shutter or aperture speed can be used to create with a camera too. Using different lenses allows the photographer to play with elements such as image exposure, lighting, and the shooting angle from which the shot is framed. This allows for some very creative photographs.

Photography is a numbers game. To come up with a great image it is preferable to take many shots with various shutter speeds, and lighting choices.

You never know which combination *(lens, exposure, point of view, or lighting)* will yield the best results. So, you take a large quantity of shots and work toward gleaning some quality results in the selection to follow.

Applying this metaphor to our quest for creative innovation. Creativity, like photography, is all about the skill of 'seeing.' Being able to approach a situation and look at it differently than everyone else.

When I was designing kitchens, I'd frequently come up with several creative approaches to remodelling a frustrating kitchen area.

Quite often I heard my clients say, **'Why didn't I THINK of that?'** Perhaps because I was looking at it with a different set of eyes and seeing the possibilities not the liabilities. I was looking for what could be, not what was!

Visit **www.SuccessPublications.ca** to order a personal copy of **Why Didn't I THINK of That?**

When we analyze a problem or opportunity, we tend to focus in on a single aspect of it, such as you would with a telephoto lens. At other times our approach may lead us to broaden our intuitive perspective and take in the bigger picture like a wide-angle lens. And at other times we see how it integrates or fits in with other factors or elements like a panoramic view would give us.

Often as a photographer you would walk around your subject seeking the best shot, the best light in which to view it or them. This procedure from a creative process in innovation can yield some fresh ideas and reflective insights.

Both the innovator and the photographer recognize the importance of quantity as an approach to quality. The best way to have a great idea is to have a great number of ideas to choose from.

A few thoughts to conclude

If you or your team are looking for methods or techniques to increase your creative output, why not take a tip from the photographic picture book. Resist the trap of looking at your current opportunities or challenges from your normal, habitual, policy driven viewpoint.

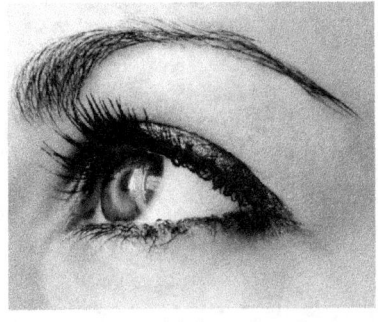

Take a *'mental'* walk around your challenge or opportunity in the context of other forces, trends, or insights. Are there similar situations you've faced or other people in your network have successfully faced in the past? What do you see? Like the photographer, examine all the variables and factors that just might lead you to a winning solution.

Remember, creativity, like photography is all about seeing or viewing things differently – about thinking and understanding fluently. Look to see the unique elements and influencing factors that other might have missed from their narrow or normal viewpoint.

"There is no doubt that creativity is the most important human resource of all. Without creativity, there would be no progress, and we would be forever repeating the same patterns."
Edward de Bono

Thunder-thinking... when lightning strikes

"The lightning spark of thought generation in the solitary mind awakens its likeness in another mind." Thomas Carlyle

Is there a way to increase my productivity and leverage my creativity?

Is it true that two minds are better than one?

Are there advantages to working with others to brainstorm my ideas, challenges, problems, and dreams?

Thunder-thinking occurs when you unleash your mind's creative power and is fully experienced when the lightning (***illumination)*** of a new idea strikes. But can this creative power be controlled or directed at will?

I've found out that simply directing and unleashing the creative power of '*several*' minds on a single issue can work miracles.

There are many **benefits to teaming up for creative problem solving.**

It can be a lot of fun and bring people closer together, providing a sense of belonging or bonding that enhances relationships and creativity. Morale can be enhanced when people are solicited for their input and ideas.

A larger number of good ideas, **better ideas**, will result if the thunder thinking process is properly utilized. Communication is often improved.

Whenever you have more than two individuals involved, team creativity or joint idea-creation can successfully be used in solving problems for most situations in family, small business, church groups, or community associations.

Webster's defines *'brainstorming'* as a group problem-solving technique that involves the spontaneous contribution of ideas from all members of the group." Alex Osborn, respected author of *"Applied Imagination,"* popularized the technique in the late 1930's.

The idea is older than that. I've been told that Hindu teachers in India practiced it over 400 years ago. It works as a part of the creative problem-solving process, occurring during the idea generation or illumination phase.

'**Thunder-thinking**' more accurately focuses this power for productive tapping into your creative genius. The creative problem-solving guide is a tri-phase process involving **fact finding**, i.e. gathering information, doing research, and defining the problem.

This is followed by the **idea generation** phase, as mentioned already.

The final phase is the **solution selection**, i.e. refining, verification of ideas and selection of the best possible alternative idea or combination of ideas.

Keep in mind that ideas generated during a 'thunder-thinking' session need to be evaluated and processed to be productive in their application.

Thunder-thinking as a creative process provides its greatest benefit in the generation of good ideas, in contrast to our experience in a typical meeting, and frequently in less time too!

The typical committee is not a breeding ground for creativity, with participants continually getting bogged down in minutia or in defending their own agenda or viewpoints.

I remember a quote that sums it up, *"God so loved the world that he didn't send a committee."*

This is not to downplay the valid contribution of committees, but to emphasize their limitations and difference in roles *unless* they are focused on creative exercises and challenging people to think and act.

Are there any rules I should be aware of, you ask?

Yes! Many, which will assist in effective thunder-thinking for your team.

Criticism and judgement are suspended ...virtually forbidden. Only by suspending judgement do we unleash the power of our individual minds and tap into the real underlying power of SYNERGY. Evaluate later.

Free thinking or wheeling is essential. No idea is too wild, too crazy, too far fetched when it comes to attacking the matter at hand. Evaluate later.

Shoot for quantity! Make it your goal to throw out as many ideas as possible. The greater number generated the greater chance of discovering a useful idea.

Work to combine and build on ideas, to improve on them, to add to them, as they are mentioned.

Encourage participants to value add or layer on the ideas of others as they seek to add new ones of their own.

Work each idea and adaptation until it reaches a natural pause and then move on to the next one.

In addition, these following **guidelines** will help you:

Make the problem to be brainstormed as specific as possible, by breaking it down into its essential components. Focus each participant's energies on a single topic. Accurate problem definition will assist in its solution being generated.

Use thunder-thinking for idea finding decisions. Judgment style decisions work better with a balance sheet or pro vs. con approach.

Once you've defined the problem to be brainstormed, **share the relevant background and parameters with all participants.**

Start each session with a **review, and a commitment by all parties to follow the basic rules and guidelines.**

Work to sidestep a "perfectionistic" atmosphere ... keep it informal and fun.

A spirit of friendly competition could be helpful.

Encourage ideas that are stimulated by previous ideas...get a chain reaction happening...feed or bounce off each other's creativity and ingenuity.

I find it helpful to appoint one 'non-participant' to act as a recorder, to ensure ideas are captured for future evaluation. Take turns if you want. This will also ensure participants are not bogged down in the recording process. Focus your energies instead on the creative process.

Avoid these common thunder-thinking blockers, i.e. phrases that kill the creative process and limit open discussion and idea generation. Be wary if you start hearing them from people on your team, family or work associates!

That is ridiculous.

We don't have the time.

That's not included in our responsibility.

Let's form a committee. (My favorite!)

What will the union (or management, or...) say?

Why change it when it's still working?

It's not in the budget!

Has anyone else tried it before?

We've never done that before.

We're not ready for that.

Add your own. Make sure you don't fall into these traps. Too often, we slip into negative thinking during a positive - creative period. This can seriously undermine the creative process!

Why does it work? Its essential success is with the chain reaction process. Idea stimulation in the host brain as well as the participant's brains. The associative power of ideas generates a two-way current.

When you offer up a new idea, your own imagination - along with everyone else's - is stimulated *(like sharing stories or jokes brings yours to mind.)*

People tend to generate more ideas with other people, in social settings, than they do individually. **Associative idea generation tests** have indicated a production increase of over 65% in social sessions, than in solo efforts.

Creative competition can work wonders, with mental output increases by up to 50%. The major difference in the concept of **thunder-thinking** is its acceptance of ALL ideas, regardless of their initial validity.

This rules out the possibility of any premature criticism or judgement stifling the creative problem-solving process. Thunder-thinking remains most effective when all participants follow the basic rules and guidelines.

Can I hold thunder-thinking or creative problem-solving sessions with only two people?

Yes, although the more the merrier. Ideally 5-10 people can become an idea generation machine. It can, however, be done with as few as two people. A good partner can stimulate effort in addition to increased associative powers.

There are a few **guidelines to keep in mind**, which apply to two-person creative teams as well as larger thunder thinking groups.

Ensure there is an incentive for each party. Work to see that values and paybacks are equitable or compatible for each of you.

Select a specific place and scheduled time to think. Allow time for each of you to rethink the problem.

Allow the information to incubate in your subconscious brain prior to each meeting.

Get together, as planned, to thunder-think the problem. Try to keep it fun and informal... bounce ideas off each other. Keep the atmosphere informal and accepting to ensure the idea flow continues. Consider each idea generated. Go for quantity and record them for future evaluation and decision. I've used a recorder (phone too) to make sure I didn't miss any good ones.

Take a break ... think alone. Review all your joint ideas to date. Do additional research and formulate your ideas.

Get back together, review ideas and generate new ones. Start choosing alternatives found satisfactory to both or all involved parties.

This is where your judgement, preferences and personal tastes come into play. This will often result in at least *'one'* solid, creative, workable idea.

Remember not to argue! This is the deathblow to the power of creative problem solving. Too many potentially good ideas die on the drawing boards or in the embryonic phase if argumentative atmospheres emerge. It's not about right and wrong ... it is about better solutions.

Intelligent discussion is great! Argument is an idea and dream killer and should be avoided at all costs. As phrased by Robert Quillen, *"Discussion is an exchange of knowledge, argument is an exchange of ignorance."*

We want to work with each other to achieve feats not grasped alone. This goal should allow us to supersede our individual egos, to reach better results in our lives.

Secret Selling Tips... Creativity can be a service focus.

Several years ago, I had lunch with the CEO of a large Canadian retail firm. I had worked with them for several years; training their VPs, helping create a book to reinforce their culture, as well as writing for their internal magazine. I had also coached and worked with their founder, **Bill Comrie**, helping him craft numerous presentations he needed to make as he garnered award after award including an honorary doctorate.

As we came to the finish of our lunch, **Kim Yost** mentioned he needed to find a way to help his 1500 salespeople across Canada become more productive, focused, and profitable.

We brainstormed ideas and in less than 15 minutes had outlined the basic idea for what we would create as our engaging online sales coaching and training **Secret Selling Tips** We launched the English version a month later and the French version shortly after that. What can you do to better serve your clients?

So, you have a problem... that's great!

So, you have a problem, that's great! Are you crazy? Actually...NO! Someone once told me that, "**I'd get paid or determine my value, by my ability to solve problems.**" That sage advice has proven to be *very profitable* over the years!

If it was easy, everyone would be doing it, and the competition would be intense. But, as most customers will tell you, most businesses are not in the problem-solving field. Your ability to solve your client's problems will be directly related to the number of sales and continued growth of your firm.

The more successfully and **creatively you and your staff solve these problems**, the more referrals, and fans you'll see. The more productive you are personally in being a solution-oriented owner, manager, or employee will dramatically affect your paycheck and career path.

I've learned to apply this **simple 4-stage process for dealing with problems**. This is an effective way to deal **creatively** with customer complaints and concerns as well as other areas of your business and life. These ideas also work with creative and strategic planning, or in everyday problem solving.

Since so many of my clients and audiences have a need to be productive in dealing with customers, I've written from that perspective. This section is excerpted from my book, **"Make ME Feel Special! - Idea-rich customer service strategies."**

Invest time in making sure you **UNDERSTAND** the problem.

The key to understanding is to **IDENTIFY** the real cause.

Take time to fully explore and **DISCUSS** all the possible solutions.
Take action to **SOLVE** or fully resolve the problem.

"The secret to Idea-rich, EFFECTIVE, Customer Service" (dealing with their problems either in advance or as they occur) is to go thru this process with your clients. After the problem has been successfully resolved, **go the extra mile**.

By that I mean, doing something unexpected to assist the client or to show them you appreciate the opportunity to prove your commitment to his wellbeing. This will help turn an angry or frustrated client into a fan, or better yet... a champion for you and your business.

Stage One: Understanding the problem: often a problem is in a perception of a difference of what we expected to happen and what happened. Here are 3 action steps to help:

Gather ALL the facts. Be thorough and investigate. Let the client talk!

Listen carefully, and don't be defensive. Wait until they've finished talking and ask more questions to draw them out, to find out their REAL concerns.

Rephrase or repeat the problem back to the client to make sure you've heard it correctly and understand what needs to be resolved. Agree on this stage.

It's important at this stage to make sure you don't fall into the trap of denying or trying to avoid the problem. Or worse yet, blaming or attacking someone else, or demonstrating the same negative emotions in response to a customer's complaint.

Just listen and get the facts!

Stage Two: Identify the Cause of the Problem: You might ask yourself or your client a few questions to find out what may have caused the problem.

What has happened? Listen and ask questions. True assessment of current situation.

What should have happened? Ask questions and listen carefully. Was perception a problem? What were they expecting?

What went wrong? This is where you start partnering with the client.

Keep in mind the true cost of an unhappy client. What future (lifetime value) purchases could you expect from this client? What future business this client could influence? What the problem at hand costs to rectify? (*Hint: average cost is 8-16 customers lost for each un-satisfied customer.*) This can be expensive.

From experience 'problems' generally often fall into **4 major areas:**

Mechanics or Function - product or service failed to work as expected.

Assembly or use - someone didn't use it correctly or put it together incorrectly.

The People Factor - we make mistakes in how we do something or how we deal with a client.

Client EGO - how this PROBLEM makes them look or feel (good or bad) in their eyes and the eyes of their friends and families.

Stage Three: Explore and DISCUSS possible solutions. This is possibly the most critical part in the client satisfaction/problem solving process.

Here is where we need to fully focus and objectively look at the challenge, we've partnered with the client to solve. Here again are a few action steps. As a leader or coach, you can follow this path with your team as well.

Suggest options. Take time to explore ALL the options that might effectively help solve this problem or at least minimize the impact.

Ask your customer for their ideas. Very often, they have a solution in mind, or have some good input that will help you mutually resolve it to their satisfaction. If they are a partner in the decision, they will help make it work and will be more inclined to be happier with the results. **Their satisfaction will result in referrals for you!**

Agree on the best solution or course of action. After you've fully explored the options, make sure you both agree on what and when you will do to resolve it.

THEN 'JUST' DO IT!

Stage Four: Take ACTION to resolve the problem. This is the completion stage that builds a foundation for a potential long-term relationship with your formerly dissatisfied client. Make this a priority focus for your firm. Once you've agreed on what needs to be done, move heaven and earth to do it, and do it better and quicker than you've promised. Remember, they are watching to make sure you were serious about making them happy. This is your chance to prove your commitment.

Again, three action steps:

Physically remove the cause of the problem or take steps to retrain if personnel.

Take corrective action to substitute, replace or repair the product or service.

Ask the client if they are satisfied with the changes and action you've taken.

Going the extra mile.

This is where you cement the relationship by doing something extra, something totally unexpected by the client. Show them you care, and are concerned about the inconvenience they've experienced. **Apply your creativity to cementing the relationship!**

Use your complaints as a creative source of product or service development. Each one is an opportunity for you to learn how to better serve your clients, refine your service or improve your product in the marketplace. This is also an opportunity to expand your business or service by using these creative solutions as stepping-stones, or business building blocks.

Yesterday's problems are today's new and improved products or services. Want to be a creativity leader? YES! Then learn from each lesson your clients give you. This is an opportunity for you to build a strong foundation for success well into the next millennium.

Don't miss the lesson. It might be a "v-e-r-y" valuable one!

A personal note from Bob

I hope to share with you some creative new approaches to problem solving or strategic planning. I appreciate the opportunity to exercise my creativity and learn together with my audiences and readers around the world, like yourself.

Often, the lessons we discuss, and the ideas generated, help me in refining my approach and my program content.

I would challenge you to use these tips and techniques in your day-to-day operations, as well as in your personal life. I think you'll find them helpful.

Remember there is always a creative solution! Share these ideas with your clients and co-workers, so they can take advantage of ways to make their lives more productive and less stressful. **Hint:** Leaders and Coaches act as catalysts and conduits for continuous learning.

I realize one of the challenges of speaking within a time frame, and having a topic that has so many variables to discuss, is covering the most relevant material. That is one of the reasons I include so much additional reference materials in my learning guides and workbooks.

I've included some Problem-solving models for your future reference and will focus on the ones that might serve you best as you begin to reframe your approach to problems that inevitably appear in your life and career. I hope you enjoy them.

Would you take a moment from time to time to share your success stories with me? This will serve several purposes. **Drop me a note at: bob@ideaman.net**

Also, you can connect with me on:

Facebook: www.facebook.com/bob.hooey

LinkedIn:
www.linkedin.com/in/canadianideamanbobhooey

YouTube: www.youtube.com/ideamanbob

Smashwords:
www.smashwords.com/profile/view/Hooey

Follow me on Twitter: @IdeamanHooey

Snail mail: Box 10, Egremont, Alberta T0A0Z0

"Without change there is no innovation, creativity, or incentive for improvement. Those who initiate change will have a better opportunity to manage the change that is inevitable." William Pollard

Break-out-of-the-box Thinking.

This will help to improve your problem-solving skills. You can create novel ideas by **NOT** following expectations, rules, regulations, assumptions or long-standing traditions or company history or policy. Go against the grain and the status quo to find the ultimate solution you need.

Just for a moment, **remove the speed limits from your mind** and challenge your traditional linear thinking. Ask yourself a few questions to trigger your creative juices.

Look at your problem or idea and ask yourself a few questions. This will allow you to change the way you look at them. A change in perspective can productively change your results.

Take a moment and ask yourself:

What if?

If only?

Why not?

Who says?

Does it apply to me?

By whose standards?

Is there another way?

Continue asking yourself:

Let's pretend for a minute we had all the resources, personnel, and time we need to solve this challenge.

What would I be able to accomplish?

Is there a second right answer?

What happens if I do nothing?

What is the best that can happen?

What is the worst that can happen?

How can I benefit or learn from this experience?

Just a few mind joggers to help kick start your thinking.

Take a few minutes and write some answers that relate to your goal or problem at hand as they relate to the previous statements and questions.

Using this style of questioning process helps **unlock your creativity**. It is this creativity that holds the seed of your eventual success in reaching your goal or resolution of your problem.

"Today... creativity must go beyond mere idea generation: the light bulb that goes on over the head of the talented person. It must become an ongoing process, not just momentary and isolated epiphanies. Creativity...is also a process that is linked to how knowledge is managed, because it is inheritantly defined by quantum leaps in understanding that lead to the realization of value."
John Kao in 'A Passion for Ideas."

Thinking in Reverse

When setting your goals, Steven Covey suggests that we should **"begin with the end in mind."** Wouldn't solving 'this' problem be a worthy goal?

Focus on the end result or desired result. Take your time and define it carefully. Ask probing, insightful questions that eventually lead you carefully, step by step, back to the current state of affairs or situation. In business it can be called reverse engineering, but it works every time.

Define your ideal solution or desired outcome. Be as accurate as you can. Keep asking yourself, **"If this is the case, what would have to happen to get this result?"** and use that as your next reverse step.

Usually, you will find the path within 10 to 12 steps.

Try it, you might just enjoy it!

1. _____ Ideal solution or outcome

2. _____ next step (backward)

3. _____next step (backward)

4. _____next step (backward)

5. _____next step (backward)

6. _____next step (backward)

7. _____present situation

Working backwards can give you fresh insights.

"Creativity is thinking up new things. Innovation is doing new things." Theodore Levitt

Ask a question… expect the answer!

Ever watch the TV game show Jeopardy, where contestants try to win by asking questions considering an answer? Sometimes the secret to solving your problem, to seeing your creativity unlocked, is in asking the *'right'* questions.

Sometimes, the simple process of *'reframing'* your problem or goal as a question will work wonders. Your mind is a wonderful tool, which we too often misjudge and underestimate. Don't be afraid to give it the stress test.

Try this following technique to unlock the creative powers of your mind in relation to reaching your goal or unlocking the solution to your problem. You can even forget it and sleep on it.

If you **frame your objective in the form of a question (???)**, and then let your mind (sub-conscious) play with it, you may just get the answer you really need.

Objective   **Question**

_____   _____
_____   _____
_____   _____

Ask a question - get an answer!

Do your homework, and whatever research is necessary to break down your problem or expand on your idea. Then let it go and sleep on it if necessary.

(Not on the job of course,☺)

Let your inner genius and Creative S.O.U.L. work on it overnight and you might be amazed at how powerful your mind really is.

The answer will come!

"The creative person wants to be a know-it-all. He wants to know about all kinds of things-ancient history, nineteenth century mathematics, current manufacturing techniques, hog futures. Because he never knows when these ideas might come together to form a new idea. It may happen six minutes later, or six months, or six years. But he has faith that it will happen." Carl Ally

Mental Vitamins and brain exercises

The mind works best when challenged with a daily routine of creative thinking, just like an exercise program designed to condition the body's muscles. The late **Earl Nightingale**, noted self-help expert, devised a very **simple method that only requires three things:**

An open mind

A pencil or pen

A pad of paper or something to write on.

Here is the system or method he devised that works as well today as it did when he introduced it to his readers and listeners.

Give your subconscious a pressing problem to digest and gnaw on just before you go to sleep. Spend 20-30 minutes thinking about a challenge, problem, or opportunity you are dealing with currently. When you lay down forget about it. While you sleep your subconscious mind, the source of most breakthrough ideas, will be mulling it over and thinking about it from various perspectives and sides.

Wake up an hour before anyone else. Find a comfortable place to sit, get a coffee or juice, a pad of paper and a pencil or pen.

Relax and let the ideas flow. Write everything down as the ideas occur, no matter how wild, far out or seemingly impractical they seem. Don't stop to edit or judge these ideas, just capture, or record them. Let your mind do a mental dump onto paper into a form you can do something with later.

This simple brainstorming method worked like a charm for Earl, on a regular basis and produced some outstanding ideas, which he later launched successfully. Some very profitable and far-reaching ideas.

According to Earl, the key is the subconscious mind which acts like a gigantic warehouse for ideas and thoughts, floating around just below our conscious mind awareness. Insights or hunches are ideas, which simply bubbled up from the vast reservoir of our subconscious mind.

In essence while you are studying or feeding your mind a problem or outlining an opportunity just before you go to sleep is like stuffing your subconscious mind. This feeds your powerful brain new fresh material to play with and from which to work.

Try this simple form of personal brainstorming… you might inspire yourself with the wisdom you draw from your subconscious mind.

Brain booster: Give your mind a workout. Try something new!

Write your name upside down — and backwards! This means you have to start with the last letter in your name. Notice how this feels.

On three telephone calls today, guess the age of the person you have talked to, right down to which day and month they were born.

"I think it's fair to say that personal computers have become the most empowering tool we've ever created. They're tools of communication, they're tools of creativity, and they can be shaped by their user." Bill Gates

Mistakes…
leverage your lessons for success!

"Crisis can often have value because it generates transformation…I have found that I always learn more from my mistakes than from my successes. If you aren't making some mistakes, you aren't taking enough chances." John Sculley

Like many of you, I hate making mistakes, and worse yet having to admit them and clean up after them. This has been, on occasion, an area of challenge for me in my growth as a person and in establishing my business. But I am learning and that is the important thing.

Someone once told me, *"Learn from the mistakes of others, you'll never live long enough to make enough of your own."* At the time, that sounded ludicrous to me, as I didn't want to admit my own, let alone discuss them with someone else, or hear about theirs.

A few years back, while flying to a speaking engagement in the USA, I read an article about a company who had tackled this *'mistake-itis'* full-on and had turned it into a **value-added training tool** for their company. What they did was invite their management and staff to submit their mistakes and each month they voted on the biggest mistake and gave a decent cash prize for the *'winner.'*

Initially I thought, *'What a dumb idea!'*

But, as I finished reading the article, I saw the wisdom in their process. What they had discovered was needless repetition of mistakes throughout the company, were costing them excessive manpower and additional resources. Someone would make a mistake, fix it, and simply continue without talking about it. In fact, the corporate climate was such that mistakes were not openly discussed. Then someone else would repeat the mistake, etc. And the costly cycle would continue.

'A mistake only proves that someone stopped talking long enough to do something.'
Michael LeBoeuf

The positive results of developing a culture where mistakes were accepted as a *normal*, even healthy part of doing the work and in making progress were amazing. But, the **sharing of the mistakes, and the lessons learned was the key point.**

Sharing the mistakes and the lessons *'leveraged'* the learning curve of their management and their staff.

It allowed them to avoid needless repetition of mistakes, and all of the lost time and costly resources that entailed.

It allowed the company to grow and expand on a stronger foundation.

It encouraged its management and staff to be more open to innovation, and to take *'educated'* risks in developing new business, services, and products to serve their changing clientele.

Food for thought...

What was your most recent mistake?

What did you learn from it?

Have you shared the lesson you learned with your team?

Do you have an organizational/corporate climate that realizes mistakes are a part of the innovation process and celebrates the lessons enroute to success?

One of my biggest lessons in life was in learning how to not *'recycle'* my mistakes. To learn from each one, savour the lesson, and move ahead boldly to make some new mistakes. And make some new progress from that process!

Interestingly enough in my role as a speaker and consultant I am now able to draw from the lessons my 'mistakes' and **not only do my audiences and clients profit from them – so do I!**

"You know, by the time you reach my age, you've made plenty of mistakes, and if you've lived your life properly, then you learn. You put things in perspective. You pull your energies together. You change. You go forward." Ronald Reagan

Success Keys from Rubbermaid

Rubbermaid is a successful company, generating 2.3 billion in retail sales. Not bad for a company who creates consumable products and take-for-granted ones for a multitude of uses.

Rubbermaid in their own words, seeks to *'Master the mundane.'* They create storage products for the house, the garage, and the patio, anywhere, something that needs to be durable, waterproof and cost effective.

Their aim in creating all of these *'mundane'* products is to promote, **"Consumer delight!"**

As I discovered, they apply the **5 Ts** in their creative design and discussion process:

Trends: Be aware of what is happening in the world.

Teams: Harness the power of applied teamwork toward a focused goal.

Training: Offer training to equip your teams to succeed.

Technology: Acquire and learn technology to make what you do easier and to expand your ability to be creative and innovative.

Creative Tension: Tension can be a good thing if applied creatively. Feed the process!

They even have **Trend Messengers** whose role is to gather information from around the world around them and share their observations with the rest of their team.

They've developed **seven success keys or operating principles**, which have helped them, reach their present success and will, no doubt, continue to do so:

Cross-functional teams are more reliably productive.

Oversight teams, drawn from the Company's top executives, supervise every business unit.

Companywide business councils focus on performance and innovation in such business practices as marketing and design.

Scrutinize market trends by keeping a close watch on surface action and digging well beneath the surface for what customers are buying, or would buy.

Don't waste time on run-of-the-mill research. Look for a need, a chance for solid impact and invest $.

Impose creative tension; inspire their people to come up with *'fresh'* solutions to new tasks in new environments.

Offer every kind of training but leave it to individual associates to take advantage of it.

Can you learn from this successful creator of home, garage, and industrial products? Can you, like Rubbermaid, investigate the world around you and see opportunities to expand what you offer your clients, and grow to the next level? My guess would be yes!

Even in a non-commercial environment, these principles would be applicable. How would you apply them in your organization?

Ask yourself:

Are you applying, or can you apply some or all these operating principles in your organization?

What would be the response from your team if you did?

Would they be more creative and able to explore opportunities for growth and innovation in your process, your products, and your services?

What do you have to lose?

When will you start this process?

I would like to thank you again for allowing me to be a part of your day and hopefully sharing some of my Ideas At Work! with your team. As we draw closer to this meeting of the minds, I would ask you to do two things for me:

Drop me a line and let me know how you've applied some of the ideas we've talked about? Would you share some of your successes with me? Write me at: **bob@ideaman.net**

Take a moment right now and answer this question? Use the space here to frame your answer:

What 'ONE' thing or idea, am I committed to doing, to exploring, to experimenting with, that I learned today?

"Creativity is putting your imagination to work, and it's produced the most extraordinary results in human culture." Ken Robinson

Thanks for reading *Creativity Counts*

 Each time I prepare to step on the stage; each time I sit down to write or in this case to re-write, I am challenged to deliver something that will be of use-it-now value to my audience/reader.

I ask myself, *"If I was reading this, what value would I be looking for?"*

As well as *"Why is this relevant to me, today?"*

These two questions help to keep me focused and clear on my objectives. They help to remind me to dig into my experiences, stories, examples, and research to provide solid information that will be of benefit and help our readers, when they apply it, succeed. That can be an exciting challenge!

I trust we have done that for you in this updated primer on more effective communication and presentation skills. *'Creativity Counts'* is my attempt to capture some of the lessons learned first-hand from observing and working with some tremendously effective leaders and to share them with you.

I'd love to hear from you and read your success stories. If you would be so kind, please drop me a quick email at: **bob@ideaman.net**

Photo of Bob in Havana

Bob 'Idea Man' Hooey
2011 Spirit of CAPS recipient
www.ideaman.net
www.HaveMouthWillTravel.com

"Creativity is… seeing something that doesn't exist already. You need to find out how you can bring it into being and that way be a playmate with God."
Michele Shea

Bob's B.E.S.T. publications

Bob is a *prolific* best-selling author who has been capturing and sharing his wisdom and experience in printed and electronic formats for the past fifteen plus years. In addition to the following publications, he has written for consumer, corporate, professional associations, trade, and on-line publications. He has been engaged to write and assist on publications by other best-selling writers and successful companies. His publications are listed to give you an idea of the scope and topics he covers.

Bob's **B**usiness **E**nhancement **S**uccess **T**ools.
Leadership, business, and career development series *(some of them)*

Running TOO Fast (8th edition 2022)

Legacy of Leadership (6th Edition 2024)

Make ME Feel Special! Idea-rich customer service strategies (2022)

Why Didn't I 'THINK' of That? (5th edition 2022)

Speaking for Success! (10th Edition 2023)

Thinking Beyond the FIRST Sale (2022)

Get to YES! - The subtle art of persuasion in negotiation

THINK Before You Ink!

Running to Win!

Bob's Pocket Wisdom series

Pocket Wisdom for Selling Professionals

Pocket Wisdom for Speakers

Pocket Wisdom for Innovators

Pocket Wisdom for Leaders – Power of One!

Pocket Wisdom for Business Builders

Additional PW books are coming in 2024

Visit: www.SuccessPublications.ca for more information on Bob's books.

"Listen to anyone with an original idea, no matter how absurd it may sound at first. If you put fences around people, you get sheep. Give people the room they need." William McKnight, 3M President

Copyright and license notes

Creativity Counts – Idea-rich success strategies

Bob 'Idea Man' Hooey, Accredited Speaker, Spirit of CAPS recipient
Prolific author of 30 plus business, leadership, and career success publications

Photos of Bob: **Dov Friedman**,
www.photographybyDov.com
Frédéric Bélot, www.fredericbelot.fr/fr
Cover Image courtesy of **Chatchai Stocker** at
FreeDigitalPhotos.net
Editorial, layout and design: **Irene Gaudet**, Vitrak
Creative Services (a division of Creativity Corner Inc.,
www.vitrakcreative.com

ISBN: 978 1 998014194 IS

Printed in the United States 10 9 8 7 6 5 4 3 2 1

"Because of their courage, their lack of fear, they (creative people) are willing to make silly mistakes. The truly creative person is one who can think crazy; such a person knows full well that many of his great ideas will prove to be worthless. The creative person is flexible; he can change as the situation changes, to break habits, to face indecision and changes in conditions without undue stress. He is not threatened by the unexpected as rigid, inflexible people are."
Frank Goble

Success Publications
a division of Creativity Corner Inc.
Box 10,
Egremont, AB
T0A 0Z0
www.successpublications.ca
Creative office: 1-780-736-0009

Visit our website for more information on these Idea-rich business success publications and other books by Bob 'Idea Man' Hooey.

We will be restructuring Success Publications (2016) to become more of a full publishing adventure to assist other authors in getting their messages on-line and in print. So, bookmark the site and come back to see who is new.

"Passion is one great force that unleashes creativity, because if you're passionate about something, then you're more willing to take risks."
Yo-Yo Ma

Acknowledgements, credits, and disclaimers

As with each of my books, a very special dedication of this piece of myself, to the two people who meant the most to me, my folks **Ron and Marge Hooey**. Sadly, both my parents left this earthly realm in 1999. I still miss our time together and your encouragement and love. I was blessed with the two of you in my life.

To my inspiring wife and professional proofreader and publications coach, **Irene Gaudet**, who loves, encourages, and supports me in my quest to continue sharing my **Ideas At Work!** across the world. Thank you seems so inadequate for your timely work in helping make my writing and my client service better! I love the time we spend together!

My thanks to the many people who have encouraged me in my growth as a leader, speaker, and engaging trainer in each area of expertise including *'Creativity Counts'*.

To my colleagues and friends in the National Speakers Association **(NSA)**, the Canadian Association of Professional Speakers **(CAPS)**, and the Global Speakers

Federation **(GSF)** who continually challenge me to strive for success and increased excellence.

To my many **Toastmasters** friends and family around the world, to whom I owe an un-payable debt of gratitude for your investment, encouragement, time, and support when I was just starting down this path; and oh, so rough around the edges.

To my great audiences, leaders, students, coaching clients, and readers across the globe who share their experiences and enjoyment of my work. Your positive and supportive feedback encourages me to keep working on additional programs and success publications like this updated version. My experience with you creates the foundation for additional real-life experiences I can take from the stage to the page, the classroom to the boardroom.

My thanks to a *select* few friends for your ongoing support and 'constructive' abuse. You know who you are. ☺

"An idea that is developed and put into action is more important than an idea that exists only as an idea." Edward de Bono

Disclaimer

We have not attempted to cite all the authorities and sources consulted in the preparation of this book. To do so would require much more space than is available. The list would include departments of various governments, libraries, industrial institutions, periodicals, and many individuals. Inspiration was drawn from many sources, including other books by the author; in this updated edition of *'Creativity Counts.'*

This book is written and designed to provide information on more effective use of your time, as a life and leadership enhancement guide. It is sold with the 'explicit' understanding that the publisher and/or the author are **not** engaged in rendering legal, accounting, or other professional services. If legal or other expert assistance is required, the services of a competent professional in your geographic area should be sought.

It is not the purpose of this book to reprint all the information that is otherwise available. Its primary purpose is to complement, amplify, and supplement other books and reference materials already available. You are encouraged to search out and study all the available material, learn as much as possible, and tailor the information to your individual needs. This will help to enhance your success in being a more effective leader or professional.

The purpose of *'Creativity Counts'* is to educate and entertain; perhaps to inform and to inspire. It is certainly to challenge its readers to learn and apply its secrets and tips, to challenge them to enhance their skills and leverage their time to create more productive outcomes.

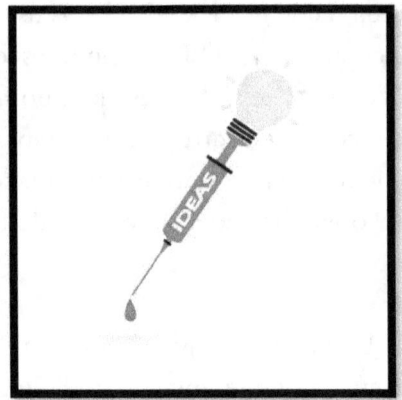

A word about the image used on the original front cover courtesy of Chatchai Stocker:

"Ideas are the life blood of business formation, growth, and long-term success.

Growing a business is everyone's role and each person on your team involved can tap into their own creativity to make that happen."
Bob 'Idea Man' Hooey

Jot down some of your ideas:

"Every day is an opportunity to be creative – the canvas is your mind, the brushes and colours are your thoughts and feelings, the panorama is your story, the complete picture is a work of art called, 'my life'. Be careful what you put on the canvas of your mind today – it matters." Innerspace

What they say about Bob 'Idea Man' Hooey

As I travel across North America, and more recently around the globe, sharing my **Ideas At Work!** *I am fortunate to get feedback and comments from my audiences and colleagues. These comments come from people who have been touched, challenged, or simply enjoyed themselves in one of my sessions.*

I'd love to come and share some ideas with your organization and teams.

"I've known Bob for several years and follow his activities in business with interest. I originally met Bob when he spoke for a Rotary Leadership Institute and got to know him better when he came to Vladivostok, Russia to speak to our leadership. **When you spoke, I thought you were one of us because you talked about our challenges just like yours.** *You could understand the others, which makes you a great speaker!"* **Andrey Konyushok**, *Rotary International District 2225 Governor 2012-2013, far eastern Russia*

"I still get comments from people about your presentation. **Only a few speakers have left an impression that lasts that long.** *You hit a spot with the tourism people."* **Janet Bell**, *Yukon Economic Forums*

"We greatly appreciate **the energy and effort you put into researching and adapting your keynote to make it more meaningful to our member councils.** *Early feedback from our delegates indicates that this year's convention was one of our most successful events yet, and we thank you for your contribution to this success."* **Larry Goodhope**, *Executive Director Alberta Association of Municipal Districts and Counties*

"Bob is one of those rare individuals who knows how to tackle obstacles in life to reach his dreams. He takes each as a learning experience and stretches for more. **His compassion and genuine interest in others make him an exceptional coach."** **Cindy Kindret, Training Manager, Silk FM Radio**

"Thank you, Bob; it is **always a pleasure to see a true professional at work.** *You have made the name 'Speaker' stand out as a truism - someone who encourages people to examine their lives and adjust. The personal stories you shared with your audience made such a great impression on everyone.*

The comments indicated you hit people right where it is important - in their hearts. *Each of those in your audience took away a new feeling of personal success and encouragement."* **Sherry Knight**, *Dimension Eleven Human Resources and Communications*

"*Without doubt,* **I have gained immeasurable self-assurance**. *Bob, your patience and your encouragement has been much appreciated.* **I strongly recommend your course to anyone looking for self-improvement and professional development.**" **Jeannie Mura**, *Human Resources Chevron Canada*

"*I am pleased to recommend Bob 'Idea Man' Hooey to any organization looking for a charismatic, confident speaker and seminar leader. I have seen Bob in action on several occasions, and he is ALWAYS on! Bob has the ability to grab his audience's attention and keep it. Quite simply,* **if Bob is involved - your program or seminar is guaranteed to succeed.**" **Maurice Laving**, *Coordinator Training and Development, London Drugs*

"*I have found* **Bob's attention to detail** *and his ability to fine tune his seminars to match the time frame and needs of the audience to be a valuable asset to our educational program.*" **Patsy Schell**, *Executive Director Surrey Chamber of Commerce*

"*Great seeing you in Cancun and congratulations on a job well done.* **The seminar was a great success! Your humorous and conversational style was a tremendous asset**. *It is my sincere hope that we can be associated again at future seminars.*" **Donald MacPherson**, *Attorney At Law, Phoenix, Arizona*

"What a great conference. It was a great pleasure meeting with you at the Ritz Carlton, Cancun and I shall look forward to hopefully welcoming you and your family in Dublin, Ireland someday." **A. Paul Ryan**, *Petronva Corporation, Dublin, Ireland*

"Congratulations on the **Spirit of CAPS Award**. *You have worked long and hard on behalf of CAPS ...***helped many speakers including me** *and richly deserve this award. Well done my friend."* **Peter Legge**, *CSP, Hof, CPAE*

"I had the pleasure of hearing and watching Bob Hooey deliver a keynote speech several years ago when he gave a presentation at a Toastmasters International Convention. **Bob impressed me greatly with his professionalism, energy, and ability to connect with his audience while giving them value.** *I heartily recommend this talented speaker and 'Idea Man' to all who want to move to the next level."* **Dr. Dilip Abayasekara**, *DTM, Accredited Speaker, Past Toastmasters International President*

"I attended **Speaking for Success** *in Edmonton.* **The mark of a true leader is someone who will lay down their own pride to teach all they know to their potential successors.** *To be taught by a man of his caliber was an honor whether you're a beginner like myself or a professional; the experience is well worth it! To Bob - it truly was an honor to meet you. Stay humble and enjoy the great success."* **Samantha McLeod**

Engage Bob for your leaders and their teams

"I have been so excited working with Bob Hooey, as he has given inspiration and motivation to our leadership team members. Both at the Brick Warehouse – Alberta and here at Art Van Furniture – Michigan; with his years of experience in working with business executives and his humorous and delightful packaging of his material, he makes learning with Bob a real joy. But most importantly, anyone who comes in contact with his material is the better for it." **Kim Yost**, CEO Art Van Furniture, former CEO The Brick

Motivate your teams, your employees, and your leaders to 'productively' grow and 'profitably' succeed!

Protect your conference investment - leverage your training dollars.

Enhance your professional career and sell more products and services.

Equip and motivate your leaders and their teams to grow and succeed, 'even' in tough times!

Leverage your time to enhance your skills, equip your teams, and better serve your clients.

Leverage your leadership and investment of time to leave a significant legacy!

Call today to engage best-selling author, award winning, inspirational leadership keynote speaker, leaders' success coach, and employee development trainer, **Bob 'Idea Man' Hooey** and his innovative, audience based, results-focused, **Ideas At Work!** for your next company, convention, leadership, staff, training, or association event. You'll be glad you did!

Call 1-780-736-0009 to connect with Bob 'Idea Man' Hooey today! Or email him at: bob@ideaman.net

"Creativity can solve almost any problem. The creative act, the defeat of habit by originality, overcomes everything." George Lois